HUMAN BODY

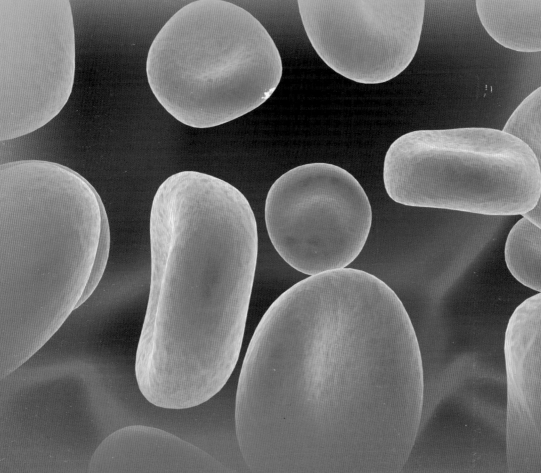

Rob Colson

This edition published in 2013 by
Franklin Watts
338 Euston Road
London NW1 3BH

Franklin Watts Australia
Level 17/207 Kent Street
Sydney NSW 2000

Produced for Franklin Watts by
Tall Tree Ltd

Editor: Jon Richards
Designer: Jonathan Vipond
Photographer: Ed Simkins
Consultant: Dr Ben Robinson

A CIP catalogue record for this book is available
from the British Library.

Dewey Classification 612

ISBN 978 1 4451 2296 0
Library eBook ISBN 978 1 4451 2244 1

Printed in China

Franklin Watts is a division of Hachette Children's
Books, an Hachette UK company.

www.hachette.co.uk

Picture credits:
Front cover: main image lucato/istockphoto, tr
Chuckaitch/Dreamstime.com, tm Sebastian
Kaulitzki/Dreamstime.com, tr Imagery Majestic/
Dreamstime.com; 1 Sebastian Kaulitzki/
Dreamstime.com, 3 istockphoto, 4 Catabar/
Dreamstime.com, 5t Antonio Ros/Dreamstime.
com, 5b Stuart Key/Dreamstime.com, 7t David
Becker/Getty, 7b Sebastian Kaulitzki/Dreamstime.
com, 8 Patrycja Kierno/Dreamstime.com, 9t
Robert Koopmans/istockphoto, 9m Sergey
Medvedev/Dreamstime.com, 10 Linda Bucklin/
Dreamstime.com, 11t Laurent Hamels/Dreamstime.
com, 12t Dannyphoto80/Dreamstime.com, 13
Warren Rosenberg/Dreamstime.com, 14
Sgcallaway1994/Dreamstime.com, 15 London_
england/Dreamstime.com, 16 Mark Sykes/Alamy ,
17t Alfonso D'agostino/Dreamstime.com, 18
istockphoto, 19t Lukasz Olek/Dreamstime.com, 19b
Vladimir Pomortsev/Dreamstime.com, 20t
Chuckaitch/Dreamstime.com, 20b David
Shankbone/GNU, 21t Paul Hakimata/istockphoto,
21b CMSP/Getty, 22 isabelle Limbach/istockphoto,
23t Ingvald Kaldhussater/Dreamstime.com, 23b
Andres Rodriguez/Dreamstime.com, 24 Marzanna
Syncerz/Dreamstime.com, 25t Ademdemir/
Dreamstime.com, 25b Drx/Dreamstime.com, 26
Jean-Marc Giboux/Contributor/Getty, 27t Klem/
GNU, 27b ARC Gritt, 28 Wacomme/Dreamstime.
com, 29t Dreamstime.com, 29b Visuals Unlimited/
Corbis

*Contents

*You are amazing

The human body is an incredibly complicated 'living machine'. It works as an integrated system – all the body's parts have to work together to keep it going.

▌Complex processes

We take our bodies for granted when they are working well, and it is easy to forget how amazing we are. Each of us is unique, but all our bodies work in the same way. Every second, thousands of separate processes are going on inside us to keep us alive and healthy. Our stomachs are digesting our food, our hearts are pumping the blood around our bodies, our muscles are responding to a never-ending stream of commands from our brains. We are not even aware that many of these processes are happening.

We are all different, but whether we are tall or short, fat or thin, the same processes are going on inside our bodies.

Working together

Many different parts of the body work together to perform a single task. Think about what you have to do when you catch a ball. First you see the ball coming towards you with your eyes. Your eyes give this information to your brain, which sends out signals to muscles all around your body to react and position the body correctly. As the ball approaches, you constantly monitor its progress and make small adjustments to your position. Your hands cup around the ball as they feel it hit the skin. If it is a hard ball, pain signals may be sent to the brain and you may have to grit your teeth to stop you dropping it.

A tennis player uses her senses to work out the shot she needs to play, then the brain sends the correct signals to the muscles to take the shot, all in a fraction of a second.

As you read, your eyes are doing a lot of work. Think about how they move and how they bring the words into focus.

Project **Your body**

List all the parts of the body that you are using when you read this book. How do they interact with each other to perform the task? Think about the signals that are being sent around your body as you read. And don't forget the effort you are making just to sit on your chair – your body is making constant adjustments to keep you seated in one place without falling over! After you have finished the book, make another list. Are there any new things on the list that you didn't know you were doing?

*Cells

Cells are the basic building blocks of the human body. We are made from over 50 trillion cells, most of them too small to see with the naked eye.

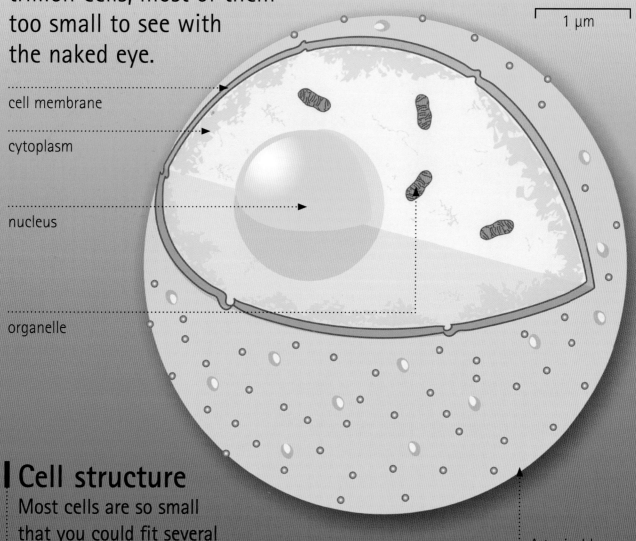

1 µm

cell membrane

cytoplasm

nucleus

organelle

A typical human cell. 1 µm = 1 millionth of a metre.

Cell structure

Most cells are so small that you could fit several hundred of them in the full stop at the end of this sentence. Each cell has an outer protective membrane. Inside the membrane are the nucleus, which contains the cell's instructions, and structures called organelles, which carry out some of those instructions. The organelles are organised into different compartments, which are held in place by a network of tiny tubes that act like the cell's skeleton.

Cell division

Cells in our bodies are constantly dying and being replaced. Skin cells, for instance, are tough and strong, but they are brushed off our bodies at a rate of 40,000 every minute. New cells are made by a process called mitosis, whereby one cell divides into two new cells. First, a copy of all the information in the cell is made. Then the cell elongates and divides in the middle, leaving a complete set of information in each new cell. By the end of our lives, 10,000 trillion cell divisions will have taken place in our bodies.

Cells from a human breast magnified 1,700 times. The cells in the centre are cancer cells, which are dividing. Cancer cells divide uncontrollably, causing potentially fatal growths called tumours.

DNA

Every cell in our bodies contains all the information it needs to turn into any other kind of cell. This information is provided by a special code held in a chemical called DNA. The complete code consists of strings of DNA called genes. We all have very similar genes, but each set of genes is unique, which is why each of us is unique. The shape of DNA was first discovered in the 1950s, and scientists are now beginning to understand how our genes interact with each other to make us who we are.

DNA is a long molecule. The code within it is arranged in twisting pairs in an arrangement called a 'double helix'.

# Organs

Cells combine with one another to make larger units called organs. Our bodies contain many organs, each performing a particular task or group of tasks.

The major organs

There are many organs in the body, but these are some of the major ones:

The heart. A powerful muscle the size of a clenched fist that pumps the blood around the body. It operates two coordinated pumps. The right side of the heart pumps blood to the lungs to be oxygenated. The left side pumps the oxygenated blood around the body. *See page 15.*

The liver. A large organ about 20 centimetres long. The liver performs over 250 different functions, the most important of which are to store sugar, to process vitamins and minerals, and to break down harmful chemicals in the body.

The intestines. A long, thin tube that absorbs the nutrients from our food, leaving the waste that we pass when we go to the loo. *See page 13.*

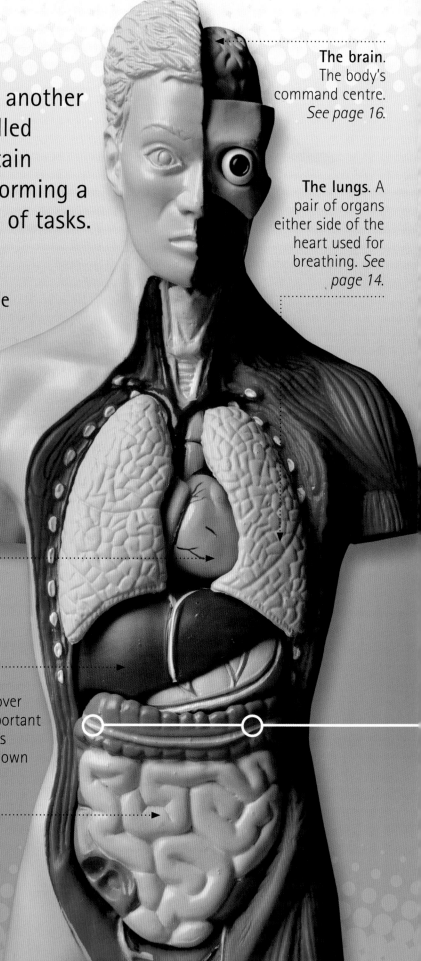

The brain. The body's command centre. *See page 16.*

The lungs. A pair of organs either side of the heart used for breathing. *See page 14.*

The skin

The largest organ in the human body isn't the liver or the brain, it is the skin. The skin is a vitally important organ, which protects us from the outside world, helps to keep us at the right temperature and, of course, gives us a sense of touch. If you could take your skin off and measure it, it would weigh over 3 kilogrammes and have a surface area of up to 2 square metres. The skin's thickness varies from 0.5 millimetres in delicate areas, such as the eyelids, to over 5 millimetres in places that need to be tough, such as the soles of the feet.

Hairs grow from the skin at places called follicles.

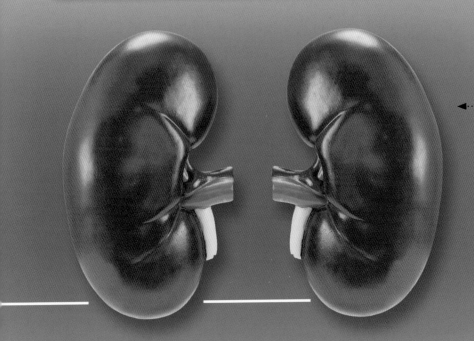

The kidneys. A pair of organs at the rear of the abdomen. The kidneys filter waste products from the blood, which are then passed from the body in the urine.

In addition to the major organs, there are many smaller ones. Our eyes are organs that we use for seeing. Our ears are organs that we use for hearing. How many other organs can you think of?

✳The skeleton and muscles

Our bodies are supported by a skeleton of strong bones. The bones are joined to each other at joints, which allow the bones to move. They are moved by muscles.

Joints

We have many different kinds of joints. Some bones, such as the skull bones, are fused together so that they do not move. These are called fixed joints. Other bones are connected at freely moving joints called synovial joints. Some joints, such as the elbow, are hinged so that the bones can only move in one direction. Other joints, such as the ball and socket joints at the shoulder and hip, allow movement in many directions, so that we can twist and turn. The bones are held together at joints by strong, flexible fibres called ligaments.

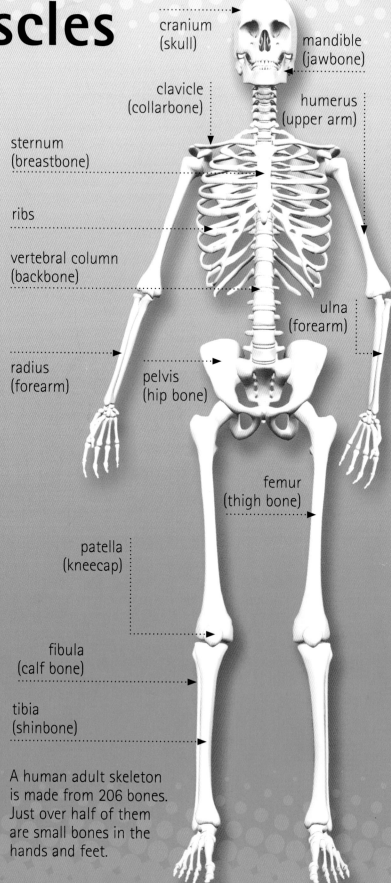

cranium (skull)

mandible (jawbone)

clavicle (collarbone)

humerus (upper arm)

sternum (breastbone)

ribs

vertebral column (backbone)

ulna (forearm)

radius (forearm)

pelvis (hip bone)

femur (thigh bone)

patella (kneecap)

fibula (calf bone)

tibia (shinbone)

A human adult skeleton is made from 206 bones. Just over half of them are small bones in the hands and feet.

Muscles

The muscles are attached to the bones by fibres called tendons. The muscles move the bones in all the directions the joints allow, but any one muscle can only pull by shortening its length, called contracting, or exert no force at all by relaxing and lengthening. Muscles cannot push. For this reason, muscles are grouped in opposing pairs, each pulling in the opposite direction. The muscle that straightens the joint is called the extensor. The muscle that bends the joint is called the flexor.

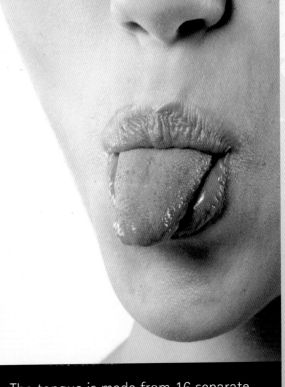

The tongue is made from 16 separate muscles that are attached to each other to allow it to make many different shapes.

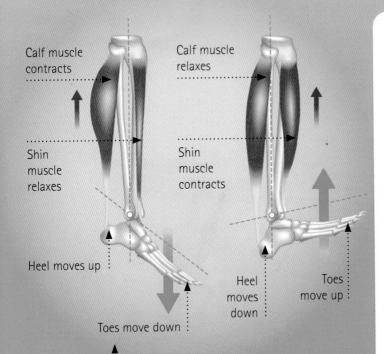

Calf muscle contracts

Calf muscle relaxes

Shin muscle relaxes

Shin muscle contracts

Heel moves up

Toes move down

Heel moves down

Toes move up

The ankle is moved up and down by a pair of opposing muscles.

Project Feel your muscles in action

You can feel for yourself how flexor and extensor muscles work together. Ask a friend to sit next to you in front of a heavy table. Ask your friend to hold the underside of the table and to push up. Feel the front and back of their upper arm. The front will be hard as the flexor muscle, called the biceps, is contracting, while the back will be soft as the extensor muscle, called the triceps, is relaxed. Now ask your friend to press down on the top of the table and feel the muscles again. Now the biceps is relaxed and the triceps is contracting.

*The digestive system

A body needs energy and nutrients to keep it going. We take in what we need from the food we eat. The process by which we extract the goodness from our food is called digestion.

Teeth

We use our teeth to bite and to chew our food and mix it with saliva (see panel). At the front of the mouth are the incisors, four at the top and four at the bottom. These are shaped like chisels for cutting. Next to the incisors are four pointed canine teeth for tearing. Behind the canines are the larger, flatter premolars and molars. Most people have eight of each of these, although some adults have 12 molars. The molars crush and grind the food. The teeth are covered in a very hard but brittle substance called enamel.

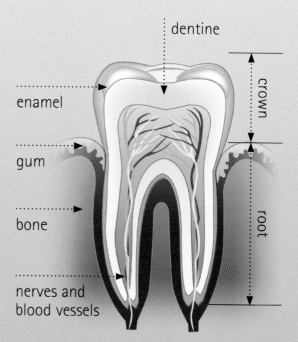

dentine

enamel

gum

bone

nerves and
blood vessels

crown

root

cross-section of a molar

(a) Before adding the iodine, the glass with the saliva (left) has already turned clear. (b) Just after adding the iodine. (c) One minute later.

(a)

(b)

(c)

Project Test your saliva

The digestive process starts in the mouth. Your saliva contains substances called enzymes that start to break down your food ready for your stomach, which is why it is important to chew your food when you eat! To see enzymes at work, fill two glasses with a solution of corn starch. Add some of your saliva to one of the solutions and leave for a few seconds. Now add one drop of iodine to each solution. The iodine reacts with starch to turn blue. In the glass without the saliva, the iodine will turn a dark blue. In the glass with the saliva, it may turn a lighter blue for a few seconds, but then the blue will disappear entirely as the saliva has already broken the starch down.

A little help from our friends!

When we swallow our food, it passes down the oesophagus into the stomach, where it is broken down by the digestive juices with the help of billions of tiny bacteria. Bacteria are single-cell organisms that live inside us but are actually separate life forms. From the stomach, the food passes into the small intestine, a long, winding tube where the nutrients are absorbed. Waste and unwanted bacteria pass into the large intestine and out through the anus. The whole process of digesting a meal takes up to 24 hours, during which time the food covers a distance of 9 metres.

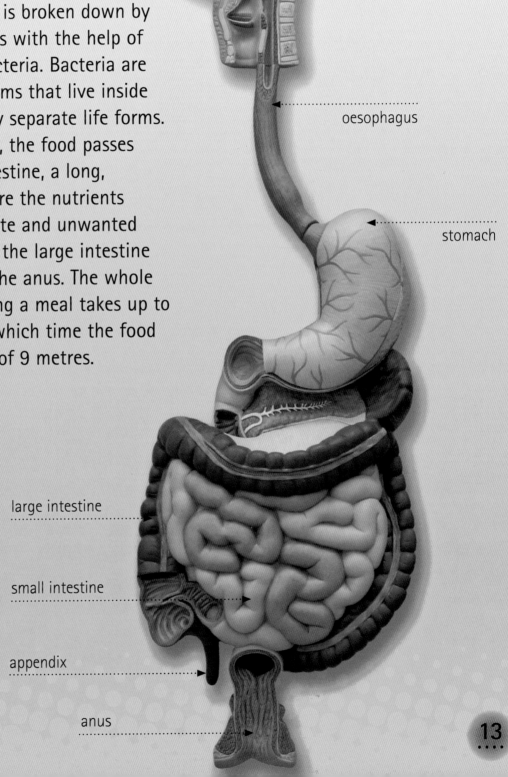

oesophagus

stomach

large intestine

small intestine

appendix

anus

The digestive system is about 9 metres long in total. The small intestine is up to 7 metres long, while the large intestine, also called the colon, is about 1.5 metres long.

*Breathing and circulation

In addition to food, the body also needs oxygen to keep it going. We take oxygen from the air, and it is pumped around the body in the blood.

Breathing

When we breathe in we take air into the lungs, which absorb oxygen from the air. The oxygen passes into the blood. The lungs take carbon dioxide, a waste gas, from the blood and put it into the air. This means that the air we breathe out has less oxygen and more carbon dioxide in it. We also use breathing to talk. As we breathe out, the air vibrates the vocal folds (cords) in the throat. By changing the shape of the mouth, we use these vibrations to make different sounds.

When we exercise, our breathing and heart rates increase to supply the muscles with enough oxygen.

Circulation

Oxygen from the lungs and nutrients from digested food are carried around the body by the blood in a process called circulation. The blood is pumped by a powerful muscle called the heart. Blood vessels (tubes) called arteries carry oxygenated blood to the muscles. Blood vessels called veins carry blood back to the lungs for more oxygen. Oxygen makes blood bright red. Blood with no oxygen is dark purple. If you look at the back of your hands, the veins just under the skin appear blue.

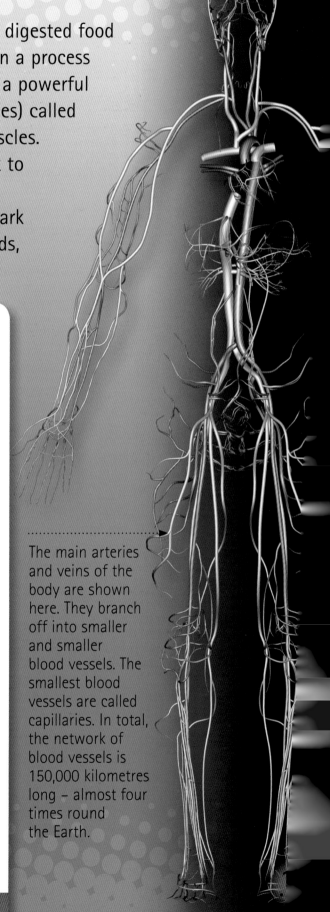

The main arteries and veins of the body are shown here. They branch off into smaller and smaller blood vessels. The smallest blood vessels are called capillaries. In total, the network of blood vessels is 150,000 kilometres long – almost four times round the Earth.

Project **Recovery time**

Sit in a chair for a minute or so and take your resting heart rate. Then run on the spot for two minutes and take your rate again. Keep taking the heart rate at minute intervals. The time it takes to return to the resting rate is called the recovery rate, and is a measure of how fit you are. If you compare your results with the results of others, you'll see that you are all different. The average adult resting rate is about 70 beats per minute. The heart rate can more than double when we exercise. Top athletes such as cyclists may have resting rates of less than 40 as they have trained their hearts to beat more powerfully.

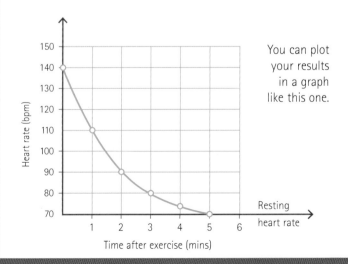

You can plot your results in a graph like this one.

*The brain

The brain is the body's control centre. The human brain is probably the most complex organ in the natural world. It communicates with the rest of the body through the nerves.

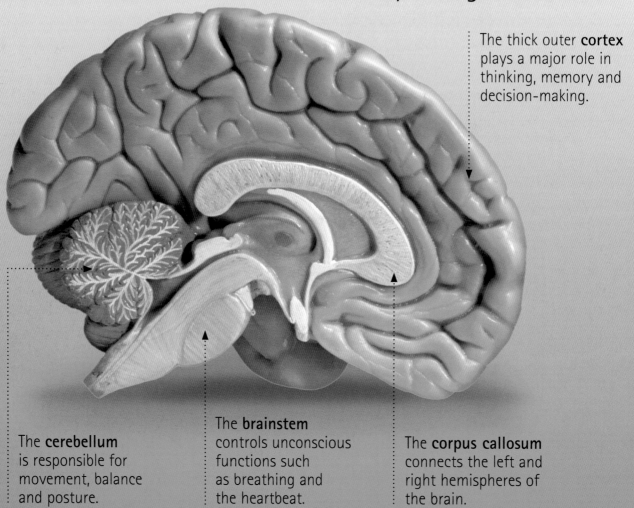

The thick outer **cortex** plays a major role in thinking, memory and decision-making.

The **cerebellum** is responsible for movement, balance and posture.

The **brainstem** controls unconscious functions such as breathing and the heartbeat.

The **corpus callosum** connects the left and right hemispheres of the brain.

All connected up

A brain contains over 100 billion nerve cells, or neurons. Each neuron is connected to up to 30,000 other neurons. There are also neurons in other parts of the body, such as the spinal cord, which control automatic movements called reflexes. Long neurons connect the brain up with the rest of the body and signals are passed along them using electricity, telling the body how to act, and also letting the brain know what the body is doing.

How we learn

The brain thinks and stores information about the past in memory. It also processes the information coming in from our senses. It takes all this information and uses it to learn. We learn by strengthening pathways between the neurons in our brains. Learning a complex new skill can take years of constant repetition so that we have the right pathways in our brains to perform it without thinking. Young children learn more quickly than older people, possibly because their brains strengthen new pathways more easily.

To become a skilled piano player takes many thousands of hours of practice.

Project Test your reaction time

Ask a friend to hold a ruler vertically in front of you. Hold your thumb and forefinger either side at the bottom. Get your friend to drop the ruler without warning you. As soon as you see the ruler drop, pinch your thumb and finger together to catch it. The time it takes you to react depends on two factors: how long your brain took to process the information from your eyes, and how long it took to send a message to your muscles. This is a measure of your reaction time. Record the point where you caught the ruler, then change over and test your friend's reaction time. Try it a few times – you may learn to get quicker!

Try to catch the ruler as soon as you see it drop.

*Hormones

The endocrine system carries messages around
the body, keeping it functioning well.
It uses special chemicals called hormones.

▮Long-term messages

The endocrine system releases hormones into the
blood from special glands. The hormones travel in
the blood to every cell in the body, but most
hormones only have messages for particular
organs. Nerves respond in a fraction
of a second, but their message is
short-lived. The messages from
hormones have longer-lasting
effects, and can affect the
body for hours, weeks or even
years. Many of the glands that
produce hormones are
controlled by a gland
at the base of the
brain called the
pituitary gland.

Hormones control
long-term development
in the body, such as
growth.

Diabetes

An organ called the pancreas produces the hormone insulin, which tells cells when to absorb glucose from the blood. Without insulin, the cells cannot absorb the glucose, which is needed for energy. Diabetes is a medical condition where the pancreas stops producing insulin or produces too little. Diabetics whose pancreas produces no insulin have to take daily injections of the hormone. Other diabetics may produce some insulin themselves and can control their condition with medicine and diet.

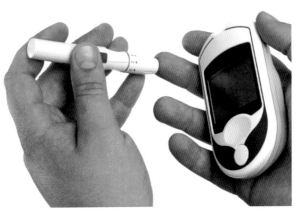

Diabetics must test the glucose level in their blood regularly to see how much insulin they need.

Fight or run away

When we are excited, scared or nervous, our bodies produce a hormone called adrenaline. Adrenaline raises our heart rate, increases the supply of oxygen and sugars to the brain and muscles, and suppresses non-essential activities such as digestion. We are now ready for action should it be required. Adrenaline helps people when they find themselves in dangerous situations, preparing them to fight or run away. We may also get an 'adrenaline rush' before an exam or when we're asked to speak in front of a large audience.

Just before the start of a race, an athlete's body produces adrenaline to ready the muscles for action.

*The senses

We use our senses to take in information from outside our bodies. We have many different senses, including a sense of temperature and balance, but the five main senses are sight, hearing, touch, taste and smell.

The eye

The eyes provide the brain with more information about the world than all the other senses put together. Light enters the eye through the lens at the front, which focuses it on light-sensitive cells on the retina at the back. The retina sends signals to the brain to tell it what the eye is seeing. The light from an object hits each eye at a slightly different angle. Our brains can tell how far away the object is by comparing the images from both eyes.

Light enters the eye through the **pupil**.

The size of the pupil is changed by the **iris** according to the brightness of the light.

The nose

Smells, or odours, are caused by very small quantities of different chemicals in the air. Odours enter the nose through the nostrils.

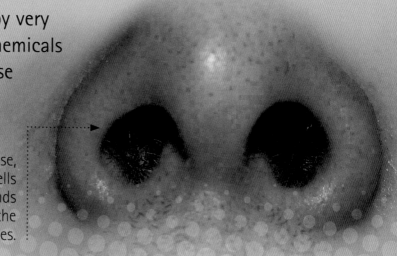

Odours dissolve in mucus inside the nose, where thousands of hair-like receptor cells identify them. Each receptor responds to one particular chemical part of the odour molecules.

Touch

Our sense of touch comes from a combination of sense receptors in the skin.

The ear

The ears detect vibrations in the air, which we hear as sound. The outer ear funnels sound waves into the inner ear, where the sound waves make the eardrum vibrate. Three tiny bones called the ossicles pick up this vibration and send it to the cochlea, which sends signals to the brain. The ear also performs the important task of keeping us balanced. The inner ear is filled with liquid, and the way this liquid responds to movement tells us what position our head is in.

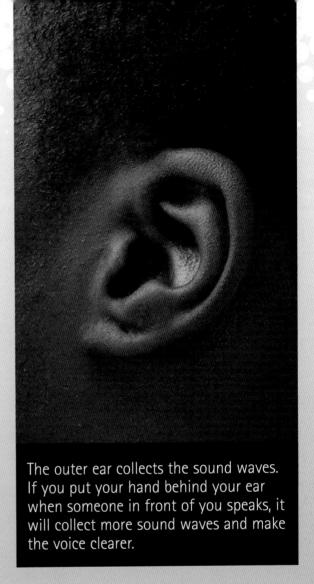

The outer ear collects the sound waves. If you put your hand behind your ear when someone in front of you speaks, it will collect more sound waves and make the voice clearer.

A close-up of the tongue shows the taste buds on the surface. A child's tongue has about 10,000 taste buds. An adult's has about half that number. The taste buds can detect five different basic tastes: sweet, salty, sour, bitter and umami (or savoury).

Project Taste test

When we eat, we use our senses of smell and sight just as much as our sense of taste. In fact, if you take away our smell and vision, it is very hard to tell what we are eating. Blindfold a friend and have someone hold their nose. Then give them a slice of pear and a slice of apple to eat. Could they tell which was which? Try them with slices of different vegetables. Our taste buds can detect basic tastes such as sweet, sour and salty, but the complex individual taste of different foods comes from our sense of smell. Take that away and we cannot tell exactly what we are eating.

*Reproduction

A new life begins after a man and a woman have sexual intercourse. The sperm of the man fertilises the egg of the woman, which attaches itself to the woman's uterus, or womb, where it starts to grow into a new human being.

Early development

Once the fertilised egg has implanted itself into the uterus, it starts to grow by cell division. It will stay here for nine months before the new baby is ready to be born. During the first eight weeks, the new life is known as an embryo as first the brain and head take shape, then the arms and legs. By the end of eight weeks, all the major organs have been formed and it looks like a tiny baby, although it is still only about 3 centimetres long. It is now called a foetus. The foetus will spend another seven months growing inside the mother, provided with all the nutrients it needs through a tube called the umbilical cord.

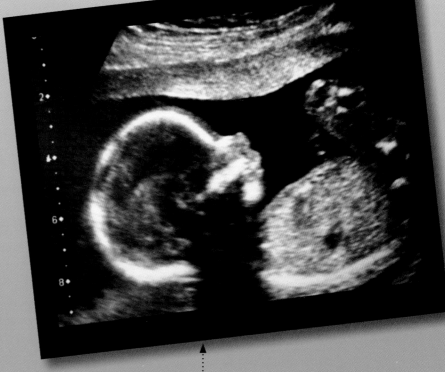

A 22-week-old foetus in its mother's womb. The image was taken using a technique called ultrasound, which uses sound frequencies that are too high to hear to form an image.

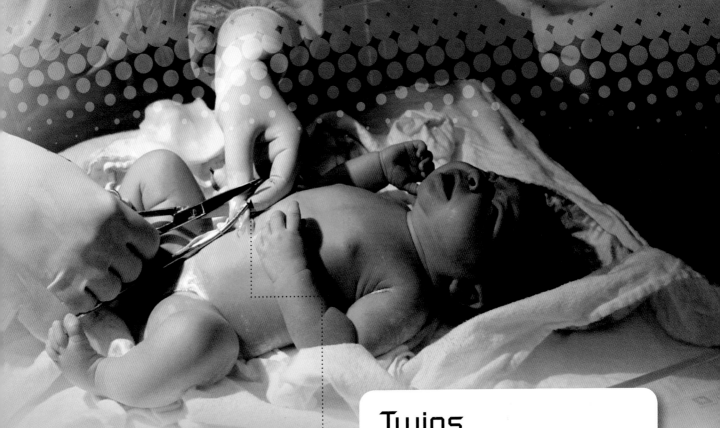

The umbilical cord is clamped and cut soon after birth to form the belly button.

The moment of birth

After nine months inside its mother, the baby is ready to be born. The process of giving birth is called labour, and it can last many hours. The mother has to push the baby out through the cervix, or neck of the womb, by contracting the muscles of the uterus. The baby usually enters the world head first, covered in a mix of blood and mucus. A cry reflex makes the baby take its first breath. Now the baby can survive in the outside world. It receives its first meal of milk from its mother's breast.

Twins

Identical twins share almost exactly the same DNA.

Usually, humans give birth to one baby at a time, but occasionally two or more are born. Twins can be made in two different ways. Non-identical twins occur when two fertilised eggs grow in the uterus. Non-identical twins may look very different and even be different sexes. Identical twins form when a single egg divides to form two embryos. Identical twins have almost exactly the same DNA so they are always the same sex and may grow up to behave in similar ways.

*The life cycle

Babies grow into adults and have children of their own. The adults grow old and eventually die, making way for the new generations of humans. This is called the life cycle.

First years

During their first years, young children grow and develop basic skills such as walking and talking. A newborn baby is totally reliant on its parents. In the first year, the eyes focus, and the baby starts first to crawl and then to walk on two legs. By the age of two, the infant will start to utter its first words. By the age of five, the young child is ready to begin school with other children. At school, children learn many of the skills they will need for adulthood.

In addition to school work, children also learn through play, as they experiment and discover more about themselves and the world.

Puberty

Physical growth is very fast in the first three years of life, then slows until a special period of growth called puberty. Puberty usually starts at the age of 10-11 in girls and 13-16 in boys. Hormones stimulate rapid growth and a series of changes that turn the child's body into an adult's body. Girls grow breasts and develop the wide hips they will need for childbirth. Boys grow more muscle and their voices become deeper. Puberty can be a difficult time for young people as their bodies change rapidly.

During puberty, many teenagers develop spots on their faces. Once their hormones have settled down, the spots disappear.

Growing old

As adults grow old, their bodies slowly start to deteriorate in a process called ageing. Some scientists believe that we are programmed to age in our DNA. Others believe that ageing is caused by the build-up of small faults in cells as they divide. The most visible sign of ageing is the change in the skin, which starts to wrinkle. Inside, the other organs are also ageing, and eventually the body dies. Older people have slower bodies than younger adults, but they are often highly valued by societies for the experience and wisdom that they have gained through their long lives.

As we age, our hair turns grey.

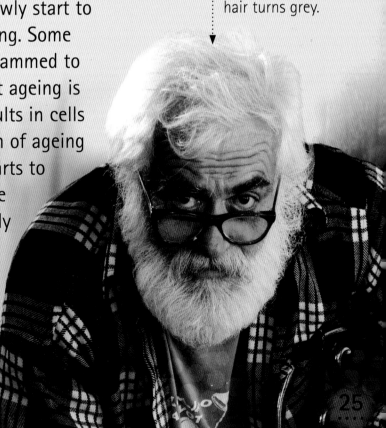

*The immune system and repair

From time to time our bodies come under attack from disease or we injure ourselves. Our immune system helps us fight off disease-carrying germs and repair ourselves.

Immune response

Damage such as a burn or a knock causes inflammation. Special cells in the blood called white blood cells surround and kill any foreign bodies, and the body makes new cells to repair the damage. Many diseases are caused by tiny bacteria or viruses called germs that get into the blood. These illnesses are fought off by proteins called antibodies, which are made by white blood cells. Once the body has produced antibodies to attack a particular germ, it is protected from future attack by them. In this way, we develop immunity to many diseases as we grow older.

When we are young, we are given vaccines that cause our bodies to produce antibodies to illnesses such as polio. The vaccines do not make us ill, but give us the immunity to fight off the disease in the future. The polio vaccine is sometimes given by mouth.

Blood clotting

When our skin is cut, we bleed, and the bleeding would continue until we died were it not for a special quality of blood called clotting. As soon as the bleeding starts, the blood begins to thicken and turn solid. Eventually it forms a scab that protects the wound and stops the bleeding. Some people have a condition called haemophilia, which means that their blood does not clot. Haemophiliacs have to be given regular doses of the substance that makes blood clot. Otherwise they could bleed to death from a simple cut.

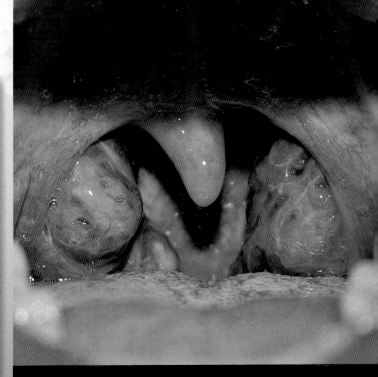
The tonsils are organs positioned either side of the back of the mouth.

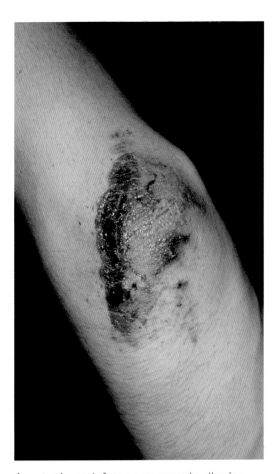
A protective scab forms over wounds, allowing the body to heal properly underneath.

First lines of defence

We are particularly vulnerable to germs through our mouth and nose. When we have a cold, our bodies produce phlegm in our nose and throat to protect us. Our saliva also contains substances that can kill bacteria that come in through the mouth. At the back of our mouths are two small organs called the tonsils. The tonsils are the first line of defence of the lymphatic system. The lymphatic system produces cells called lymphocytes in a special fluid called lymph, which also kills invading germs.

*Keeping healthy

Our bodies are amazing but there are certain things that we need to do to keep them working well, including resting them with regular sleep. We also need to eat the right food and take exercise.

A healthy diet

A good diet keeps us fit and prevents diseases such as heart disease, diabetes and cancer. We need to take in a wide range of nutrients and vitamins through our food. Most of these are contained in fresh fruit and vegetables, and we should eat plenty of these every day. Food such as pasta and potatoes contains carbohydrates, which give us energy. Food such as meat, fish and pulses contains protein, which we need to grow and repair our bodies. We should avoid eating too much fat, sugar or salt, which can make us overweight and clog up our arteries.

This is a healthy meal, with a mix of fresh vegetables and lean meat.

Keeping fit

Regular exercise strengthens the muscles and the heart and keeps us from becoming overweight. There are three main kinds of exercise. Stretching exercise, such as yoga, is good for our joints and keeps us flexible. Aerobic exercise, such as cycling, swimming or jogging, makes us out of breath and is good for our hearts. Anaerobic exercise, such as weight training or sprinting, increases our muscle size and strength.

Swimming is a very good aerobic exercise that uses many different muscle groups. The water supports the body in a way that minimises the risk of injury.

Bad habits

Bad habits such as eating too many sweets, drinking too much alcohol or smoking do your body serious damage. Eating a lot of sugar damages the teeth and over many years can also lead to heart disease. An adult can drink alcohol in moderation, but drinking too much damages the liver and other major organs. Smoking is a particularly damaging habit. It causes lung cancer, heart disease and many other conditions, and the second-hand smoke can damage the health of others around you. Smoking is addictive, which means that it is hard to stop once you've started, so don't start!

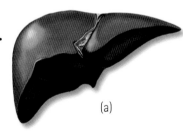

(a)

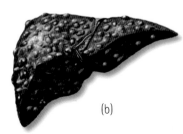

(b)

Alcohol is broken down in the body by the liver. Drinking too much alcohol can cause the disease cirrhosis. Liver (a) is a healthy liver. Liver (b) has scars on it caused by cirrhosis.

*Glossary

Abdomen
The part of the body between the chest and the hips that contains the digestive system.

Absorb
To take into the body substances such as nutrients and water.

Blood vessels
Tubes that carry blood around the body. There are three main kinds of blood vessel: arteries, veins and capillaries.

Cancer
A disease caused by the uncontrolled division of cells.

Carbohydrate
A chemical in food, such as sugars and starch, that gives us energy.

Digestive juices
Acidic liquid in the stomach that breaks down food.

Elongate
To increase in length.

Enzyme
Protein that speeds up a chemical reaction.

Gene
A sequence of DNA that tells a cell to behave in a particular way.

Gland
An organ that puts chemicals such as hormones into the bloodstream.

Inflammation
A reaction of the body to injury or disease, which causes swelling.

Mucus
A slimy liquid made in parts of the body such as the nose or the stomach.

Oxygenate
To fill with oxygen.

Suppress
To prevent or keep to a minimum. Adrenaline suppresses digestion.

Vibrate
To move rapidly backwards and forwards around a central point. The vocal folds (also called vocal cords) vibrate to make sounds.

Vitamin
A chemical in food that the body needs to keep it healthy.

*Resources

The Human Body Book,
by Steve Parker (DK, 2007)
A comprehensive exploration of the
body and the ways it can go wrong.

Making Sense of Science:
The Human Body, by Peter Riley
(Franklin Watts, 2008)
A guide to the history behind the
science, with ideas for experiments.

Dr Frankenstein's Human Body Book,
by Richard Walker (DK, 2008)
Learn how a body fits together as you
help Frankenstein build his monster.

Oxford Children's A To Z to the
Human body (OUP, 2003)
Illustrated explanations of over
300 different terms used in biology.

The Body Owner's Handbook,
by Nick Arnold (Scholastic, 2009)
A Horrible Science guide to the body
and how to look after it.

Human Body: Eyewitness
Project Book (DK, 2008)
A compendium of project ideas on
every aspect of the human body that
you can do at home.

Websites

www.sciencemuseum.org.uk
The website of London's Science Museum,
with features on medicine, the brain and the
cycle of life.

www.sciencewithme.com
Games and science project ideas, with
worksheets and colouring books to print out.

www.learnenglishkids.britishcouncil.org/
en/category/topics/human-body
Interactive games, exercises and quizzes.

www.childrensuniversity.manchester.ac.uk
Scientists from the University of Manchester
answer questions about the human body,
health and medicines.

www.gosh.nhs.uk/children/
general-health-advice/body-tour/
A virtual tour around the human body, from
Great Ormond Street Hospital. Click a body
part for more information and surprising
facts and trivia.

Please note: every effort has been made by the publishers to ensure that these websites contain no inappropriate or
offensive material. However, because of the nature of the Internet, it is impossible to guarantee that the contents of
these sites will not be altered. We strongly advise that Internet access is supervised by a responsible adult.

*Index